Receptive Language Difficulties

**Practical strategies
to help children
understand spoken language**

Liz Baldwin

Permission to photocopy

This book contains materials which may be reproduced by photocopier or other means for use by the purchaser. The permission is granted on the understanding that these copies will be used within the educational establishment of the purchaser. The book and all its contents remain copyright. Copies may be made without reference to the publisher or the licensing scheme for the making of photocopies operated by the Publishers' Licensing Agency.

Receptive Language Difficulties

MT10778

ISBN-13: 978 1 85503 441 9

© Liz Baldwin

Illustrations © Matt Ward

All rights reserved

First published 2008

Printed in the UK for LDA

Abbeygate House, East Road, Cambridge, CB1 1DB, UK

Contents

Introduction

Receptive language difficulties (RLD) are a hidden disability. Children with RLD easily go unnoticed. As a result they frequently struggle through school, failing to achieve their potential and often confused and unhappy.

In any one class of thirty children you can expect to find between one and three with some form of speech and language difficulty. The children with speech-sound and spoken-language problems are usually easy to spot: you can hear the difficulties they are having and see the impact on their communication that this is having. Children with RLD are harder to identify: their spoken language may be adequate and they may develop strategies and behaviours to mask their confusion with language.

This book will help you:

- understand the nature of receptive language
- identify children with RLD
- consider the impact of RLD on learning and social skills, including behaviour.

It will give you practical strategies to improve children's:

- listening skills
- vocabulary-learning skills
- self-help skills.

In addition, it will provide you with tips and ideas to make your classroom language friendly.

Children may experience RLD throughout their school life and beyond. The principles discussed in this book are appropriate for pupils from Foundation Stage through to Key Stage 4. The strategies and activities are primarily aimed for use with children in Key Stages 1, 2 and 3. Thoughtful adaptation of the language used and expectations of the children will enable them to be used with children in Foundation Stage and Key Stage 4 as well.

The book provides a balance of theoretical and practical information, considering RLD in the context of the development of language and social skills. It is my experience, from working with staff and parents, that once the nature of the children's difficulties is understood, the solutions become more obvious.

The book contains photocopiable resources and pro formas for activities. There are checklists for the identification of children with RLD and reflection on classroom practice. Each of the chapters giving practical strategies has activities that can be delivered to the whole class or smaller groups. These may also form the basis of individual programmes of work for children who require more specialist intervention.

The book is useful for staff working in mainstream and special education: class teachers, SENCos and teaching assistants. Speech and language therapists will find it provides them with useful material to recommend and discuss with teaching colleagues. It will also help parents understand the nature of their child's difficulties and how these will affect them at school.

This publication is an outcome of nearly twenty years' experience working in a variety of mainstream settings, supporting children and young people, their parents and the staff who work with them. Working with and for children with RLD is a team effort, and I am grateful for all I have learned from the many people I have met along the way.

I hope you will find this book a valuable addition to your toolkit as you endeavour to support and encourage children with RLD.

Chapter 1

What is involved in understanding spoken language?

Understanding spoken language is a complex skill, learned over the years of early development. We perhaps only notice the complexity of it when things appear to go wrong in a conversation or dialogue. This chapter sets out some of the skills children acquire while developing effective understanding of spoken language. These skills are used later to understand written language.

As you read the next few pages, try to have in mind one or two children whom you think have understanding difficulties. This will personalise the aspects that are being discussed. The examples may stimulate you to think of particular children you have encountered.

Spoken communication is concerned with information conveyed through words (verbal) and other means (non-verbal). Both elements carry information that is vital to understanding the message being communicated. The following pages identify these elements.

Verbal understanding

Think about spoken language. It is a string of sound that we listen to and decode. Consider a language that is totally unfamiliar. You hear the musical tones and perhaps pick out some speech sounds. You will not find it possible to separate out individual words, and you are unlikely to gain any meaning from what is said. In this chapter you will discover the skills necessary to gain all the relevant information from a string of sound.

Early attention to spoken language

From birth infants tune in to their mother's voice. They recognise and distinguish familiar and unfamiliar voices, then familiar phrases and words. For example:

- ☐ the word 'teddy' always being used in reference to the soft blue toy that a baby brother or sister cuddles
- ☐ 'Mummy's home' being used at a time of lots of cuddles and smiles.

Very young children learn to associate language with meaningful events or objects. From the age of 12 months they start to break down the strings of sounds they hear.

Phonic analysis

To be able to attach meaning to individual words, we need to be able to distinguish one word from another. Some words sound very alike – for example *work* and *worm*. From early infancy the ability to listen to words and pay attention to the sounds within is fundamental. The skill of phonic breakdown precedes any knowledge of letters (graphemes). As adults we are influenced by how we think we would spell a word. Young children focus on storing what the word sounds like.

When a word is heard for the first time, we go through a quick phonic analysis: what sounds did I hear in that word? The word is then stored in short-term memory, coded with those sounds. Then we compare it with other words stored in our memory bank (lexicon) and see if it matches. If it does, we assume it is a familiar word and take the meaning from the word previously stored.

Often the initial hearing and storage of a word is incomplete. Think about when you hear a new word. You may ask for it to be repeated. You are trying to get its sound properties fixed in your memory. It is easy to see how meanings become confused with similar-sounding words, and how real difficulties arise for children for whom phonic analysis is a problem.

Vocabulary

Having heard a new word and stored what it sounds like, we need to find out what it means. How do we do this? Children do not go to dictionaries and look up the meaning of new words every time they hear one; nor do we, as adults, do this most of the time. We pick up meaning from hearing a word many times in context.

For example, a young child hears the word *ball* every time the round red thing is rolled to them or they pick it up and throw it around. At first the word *ball* will apply only to their particular thing, but then they will hear and notice the word being used for the round thing on television that lots of people are kicking, and for their friend's thing that is a different colour, and for those round things in the book that Dad reads to them.

See how the meaning is gradually acquired and broadened as they hear the word in different contexts. You will understand how this works for you when picking up new words. As language develops it changes, and new words are introduced and understood long before they enter the *Oxford English Dictionary*. How did you come to understand what they meant?

The gradual acquisition of meaning is more difficult for children who are not good at phonic analysis and storage. Each time they hear a new word they may store it separately, rather than recognising that what they have heard is the same as one already stored. This is explored further in Chapter 2.

Semantics

Having acquired the meanings of individual words, we have to appreciate that when words are put together they affect the meaning of each other. Words do not stand in isolation. They are put into sentences and phrases and need to be understood within this context, otherwise meaning is lost. For example, think of the meaning of the word *coffee* in the following:

◯ a strong black coffee
◯ a slice of coffee cake
◯ a coffee-coloured sofa.

To understand these, you have to bring meaning from the word *coffee* and apply it to the other words. It is like mixing two colours making a new but related colour.

We learn to recognise that verbs change objects:	Adverbs change verbs:
The boy is crying. The boy is reading.	The leaves fell silently. The leaves fell quickly.
Adjectives change nouns:	A negative word affects whether something is present or not:
the tiny clown the scary clown	There is no more milk. The snow has gone.

When we consider a child's ability to understand, we must not assess their skills simply on the basis of whether they can understand a series of individual words. The meanings of words have to be seen in the context in which they are said or written.

Syntax

In addition to the words used, information is conveyed in sentence structures. Syntax is the sentence structure we put our words into. Through changes in the way literacy is now taught we have become more aware of grammatical structures. The ability to take meaning from the syntactic elements of spoken language precedes that skill in written text. For example:

◯ The Vikings invaded Britain.   ◯ Britain was invaded by the Vikings.

The second of these sentences is a reversible passive, and changes the usual grammatical rule that meaning follows word order. If we pick out the key words in sentences we can normally understand what is being said. In the first sentence, the key words are *Vikings, invaded, Britain*. The meaning remains intact. In the second sentence, picking out key words results in understanding the opposite of what is intended: *Britain, invaded, Vikings*.

Similarly, the presence of question words changes our understanding of what is said, and subsequently what is required from us in response, as in these examples:

'Where is the train going?' *vs* 'The train is going.' *vs* 'Is the train going?'
'Who is the girl on the swings?' *vs* 'The girl on the swings.' *vs* 'Is the girl on the swings?'

Morphology

Word endings and small grammatical words such as *he, she, they* carry information which helps us understand the full meaning of what is being said. These include the following:

- ☐ verb tense markers: -ed (past tense), going to (future tense)
- ☐ plural 's' marker: houses, pencils
- ☐ possessive 's' marker: Sam's book.

All these elements carry information that the listener needs to be able to interpret in order to gain a full understanding of what is being said.

Example

Look at these two 'sentences' using nonsense words. Can you answer the questions?

The stapes glopped on the lan. They jutly meered at the shib.

What did the stapes do?   How did the stapes meer?
Where did the stapes glop?   Where did the stapes meer?

You were able to work out the answers using your knowledge of syntax and morphology. Did you understand the full text? No, because some of it is using unfamiliar vocabulary.

To conclude this information about verbal understanding, remember that effective understanding comes from bringing together a number of elements. Understanding spoken language is a complex skill. In Chapter 2 we shall see how this skill breaks down for some children and the impact of that on their communication skills, and on their social and learning skills.

Non-verbal understanding

It is easy to overlook non-verbal understanding. However, research has concluded that we pay more attention to the non-verbal aspects of communication than we do to the words that people use. Whilst we might distrust the words that someone uses when talking to us, we tend to believe the message conveyed by the way they say it. Have you ever come away from a conversation feeling a little uneasy because what someone said did not match their non-verbal communication?

Children have to learn to interpret the messages conveyed by non-verbal information just as they have to learn about vocabulary and morphology. Information is conveyed in a variety of ways, and they have to learn to understand it.

Intonation

When we talk, we usually do so with a musical lilt to our voices. This is intonation, and it conveys a great deal of information. Try saying the following sentence in the three ways suggested; don't change volume, just alter your intonation: 'Children, put your books away.'

☐ Happily, carefree   ☐ angrily   ☐ sleepily.

Our response to what someone says is affected by the way in which they say it. If the children detect that you are making a request happily they will probably respond in a happy way. If they have detected that you are angry, the manner of their response will change. It is possible that when children do not respond as we would consider appropriate, it is because they have not understood the full message being communicated by the combination of words and intonation.

To appreciate sarcasm, we need to be able to understand intonation. The intonation will betray that something is being said sarcastically and so convey the opposite meaning. Try saying the following sentences genuinely and then sarcastically. Listen carefully to your intonation:

☐ 'I really like coming to school.'   ☐ 'That was a great piece of homework, Craig.'

Volume

Volume is similar to intonation in that it can convey how someone is feeling. It is also used to convey levels of intimacy between friends. We may whisper something or lower our voice with a friend, but this would not be appropriate with a boss or a stranger.

Facial expression

Our faces give away a lot of information which is vital to understanding the full message. This is why a conversation on the phone is different from one that is face to face. Children have to learn to look for and recognise the facial signs. At first they will be able to distinguish only between happy and sad expressions. As adults we can detect a huge range of emotions from faces, especially from eyes. You might like to try standing in front of a mirror, then covering your face, apart from your eyes, with your hand. Now make some expressions: surprised, worried, shocked, furious, sleepy, contented. Your eyes give it all away.

It is possible to pay too much attention to children who do not give eye contact all the time. In fact, when listening and when speaking we look for a short time and then look away; anything more than this can make us feel uncomfortable and constitutes staring. Interestingly, staring is also conveying some information in a non-verbal way; it can be considered obtrusive or flirtatious.

There is also information to be gained from watching eye gaze – looking at whatever the speaker is looking at. If, for instance, the speaker is talking about the chairs in the hall, they are likely to be looking at the chairs or in the direction of the hall. Children who cannot follow the spoken language very well will quickly pick up the clues from your eyes to help them understand you. When giving instructions we often use eye pointing to supplement our talk. For example:

'Copy what is on the whiteboard [*looking at the whiteboard*] into your
homework diaries [*looking at children's books*].'

Posture

As with facial expression, a considerable amount of non-verbal information is conveyed through our bodies. Children have to learn to notice the signs and to be able to understand them. Consider how you know whether someone is feeling relaxed, worried or angry just by the way they look: you look at the position of arms and legs, and head tilt. There is also information to be understood by proximity – how close it is appropriate to be to someone. Understanding proximity gives you clues about friendships and relationships. These are complex skills to learn, but older children will be able to pick up the clues.

Gesture

Gesture accompanies our talking, even when the person we are talking to cannot see us. (Watch people on the phone: their hands may be moving all over the place.) It conveys emotions; for example:

- ☐ 'Come here' while beckoning
- ☐ exasperation, with hands on hips.

We often also point to what we are talking about with our hands, in a similar way to using eye gaze. For example:

- ☐ 'You need to use the computer in the corner of the room' [whilst pointing]
- ☐ 'You've got some chocolate on the side of your mouth' [whilst pointing].

Gesture acts as a supplement to spoken words and may provide valuable clues for a child who cannot understand the words. Think of the common gestures for the following:

- ☐ Where is it?
- ☐ Give it to me.
- ☐ Stop that now.
- ☐ I don't know.

Summary

Non-verbal information helps children when they do not understand the verbal information. Think of yourself in a country where you do not understand the language – the same would apply to you. This is a normal part of language development. Think about the gestures, intonation and facial expressions we use with infants to supplement our talking. We are giving non-verbal clues to help them understand the verbal information given alongside.

We have seen that understanding spoken language is a complex skill that brings together phonics, vocabulary, semantics, syntax, morphology and various non-verbal elements.

In the next chapter we shall look at how these skills come together to ensure effective communication through a simple model of language.

Chapter 2

Difficulties in understanding spoken language

In Chapter 1 we looked at the component parts that are necessary for understanding spoken language. We now need to draw these elements together and consider how they operate within the communication process. Communication requires at least two participants: a speaker and a listener. When one has spoken and the other has listened, the roles are reversed as the listener becomes the speaker and the speaker listens. It is most useful to look at this as a cyclical process.

In this chapter we shall consider a model for language and look at the impact of each stage on the next. We shall then look at how this can break down, resulting in receptive language impairment.

The communication cycle

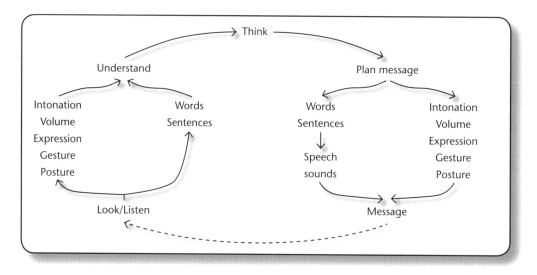

As we look at the cycle of communication it is useful to have a scenario in mind. Let us say that Priti has just come into the room and started up a conversation with her friend Jason.

> 'Hi, Jason. I didn't go to the football last night.'

As Priti starts to speak, Jason has to listen and give his attention to Priti. He will probably look at her. In doing this he is gaining some non-verbal information from Priti, such as facial expression.

- ☐ How does she look as she is telling him the information?
- ☐ Does this support the language she is using?

Jason's looking gives Priti some listener feedback and tells her that he is listening to what she is saying – that she has gained his attention. So the first element of the cycle is to **look and listen**.

There is both **non-verbal** and **verbal** information to be gained.

Jason will listen for:
- ☐ words
- ☐ sentence types
- ☐ intonation and volume.

He will watch for information from:
- ☐ facial expression
- ☐ gesture
- ☐ body posture.

Having gathered this information, Jason needs to be able to interpret it all, to understand or to make sense of the information he has gathered, having watched and listened.

So far the cycle has been concerned with gathering information. This stage is referred to as **receptive language** or **input**.

Jason has to think about the information gathered and his interpretation of it, in order to gather some meaning from what Priti has said. Only then does he plan his response.

Jason will first plan what he wants to say, and then how he wants to say it – the non-verbal and verbal elements he will use in order to convey his message. He will plan this in the light of what he understands Priti to have communicated to him and his knowledge of the context. This stage is referred to as **expressive language** or **output**.

The roles reverse and Jason becomes the speaker, whilst Priti listens. Jason responds.

'Oh, that's great! What did you do instead?'

Priti says, 'We went to the cinema, which is what I wanted to do in the first place', and the communication cycle continues.

Jason's response was made appropriate because he was able to receive the input given by Priti, take meaning from it (process it) and then plan and deliver an appropriate response in the light of the fact that he knows Priti hates watching football (using his prior knowledge).

The reason for showing this communication process as a cycle is to make plain how each element is dependent on the preceding elements. If Jason had not given Priti his attention when she spoke to him, he would have failed to gather all the information he required in order to make an appropriate response. He might have gained only some of the input. For example, if Jason failed to gather some non-verbal information, missing Priti's facial expression of joy and relief, he may have responded, 'Oh, that's a shame.' If he had not understood the negative in Priti's sentence, he would have responded to her on the basis of thinking she had been to the football.

If Jason had not used his knowledge of Priti's dislike of football, and thought only of his own love of football, his response would have been different.

What we can pick up from this interaction is that we may become aware of breakdown in receptive language only by looking at the appropriateness or otherwise of the response or output.

Receptive language impairment

We shall now consider the nature of receptive language impairment (RLI). Children with this difficulty may have an overarching problem with gathering and processing information given in a communication context. Alternatively, they may have a specific difficulty with one element of the cycle. Let us consider each element and the consequences of breakdown at each level.

Listening and attention

Children may have difficulty in attending to spoken language. Many children with poor receptive language skills also have poor listening skills. That has a direct effect on their ability to gather the information given in an interaction. As we have seen, failure to attend to a stimulus results in faulty understanding and consequent inappropriate response (see Chapter 5). If children do not hear, or mishear, they will plan and deliver a response that is based on misinformation. This earliest element of the cycle is an essential focus when working with children with RLI. Sometimes improving the child's ability to listen and to give focused attention to what is being said brings about a remarkable improvement in their responses. This suggests that the child's difficulty was not to do with language but was instead a listening and attention problem.

Non-verbal and verbal information

A breakdown at this level results in the child listening appropriately but being unable to gather the information presented to them, and then being unable to make sense of it. The child may have poor memory skills and find it hard to retain what has been said long enough to break it into its constituent parts (dialogue to sentences, sentences to words, words to phonemes). The consequence of this is that the information that the child has available to be processed at a different level of the cycle is faulty or patchy. Children may have a specific difficulty affecting their ability to gain meaning from vocabulary, or from syntax and morphology (see Chapter 1). Some children find it hard to interpret non-verbal information.

Language processing

The child with RLI will have problems at the level of processing, where all the information gathered is interpreted. Children appear to be slow to process what has been said. Sometimes extra time to plan a response is helpful. Other children are trying to interpret a half message as they did not gather the full amount of information. Children who struggle with interpreting language have a harder task if they do not have all the information available to them.

RLI and output problems

As has been demonstrated by the communication cycle, it is probable that a child with RLI will be identified by output errors. Their responses show that they have not understood what has been said, or that certain elements of communication carry little meaning for them. This is particularly noticeable with non-verbal communication. If a child cannot gain meaning from intonation, facial expression, and so on, they are unlikely to use these appropriately themselves.

The root of an output difficulty often lies in the input area. This is why emphasis is put on helping to improve receptive language skills. It is also why RLI is a hidden difficulty: there tends to be an assumption that the difficulties lie with a child's output, when the root is in the input.

RLI and communication skills

The development of spoken language relies on children giving their full attention to language, developing an understanding of that word, or phrase, or grammatical structure, and then using it in their own talking. As a rule understanding precedes use in talking. When a child appears to have poor use, or a poor range, of spoken vocabulary, the likelihood is that they have a poor understanding of vocabulary and that is why they do not use these words in their own talking. For example:

> 'I want that thing over there.'
> 'I'm going to that place. You know. Over there.'

These examples show how they may overuse non-specific words because they do not have the vocabulary to use, but do have the ideas they want to convey.

Here the child described a pony. They did not know the word, but knew it wasn't just a horse.

> 'It's a little horse.'

Similarly, a child using grammatical immaturities or omitting grammatical markers may not understand the more complex structures, and so is unable to use them. For example:

> 'That girl look at mouses. He like mouses.'

Here the speaker is demonstrating a number of grammatical errors:

- ☐ confusion between the personal pronouns *he* and *she*
- ☐ omission of verb tense information ('That girl looked', or 'is looking'.)
- ☐ simplification of the use of plurals, which suggests a failure to understand the meaning conveyed in the irregular plural *mice*.

Effective intervention and support for the child will depend on the cause.

Just as there are children with specific RLI, there are children with well-developed receptive language skills whose expressive language is impaired. This is not the subject of this book. It is important to note that children may present with similar output problems whilst having different underlying deficits – hence the need for thorough investigation if intervention is to be successful.

RLI and social skills

The child with RLI may be at risk of difficulties in social relationships. These children may become isolated because they cannot keep up with the spoken language expectations of their peers. They get left behind in play because they cannot understand the ideas their friends are expressing, or cannot respond and add to them, because of their spoken language deficits. Children with RLI may prefer the company of adults because they are more accommodating than peers in terms of differentiating their language, being patient in waiting for responses, and accepting errors.

As the children grow older the verbal banter that occurs between friends becomes increasingly hard to keep up with. Jokes are particularly hard to understand as they rely on complex understanding of vocabulary (often knowing double meanings of words, or other subtle linguistic nuances). Children may be unable to assert themselves verbally in social situations as this requires fast processing of the context and an appropriate response. In such circumstances children may resort to physical ways of responding, such as hitting out, pushing or isolating themselves to avoid a potentially difficult situation. (For more information about RLI and behaviour see Chapter 4.)

As mentioned earlier in this chapter, children who do not use some of the non-verbal elements of communication appropriately are likely to be unable to understand the information they convey. This difficulty is with the area known as **pragmatics**. Children with pragmatic difficulties are those who have problems with the social use of language. These children may not understand the rules of conversation and interaction concerning:

- ○ waiting their turn
- ○ topic maintenance
- ○ understanding what information a listener needs and what information is redundant.

Intervention for this group of children needs to be based not only on practising appropriate skills of interaction, but also on developing an understanding of the need for the rules. Whilst these difficulties are part of the collection of difficulties experienced by children and adults with autism and Asperger syndrome, they may be present in children with RLI.

RLI and literacy

Without question the biggest danger faced by children with RLI in regard to literacy development is that though they learn to read, they do so without taking meaning from print. In the first few years of a child's acquiring reading skills this may go unchecked. With more emphasis on comprehension of text within literacy testing, these difficulties are now being identified earlier.

The dangers for the child are these:

They fail to develop an intrinsic enjoyment of reading. This is like being able to read a foreign language out loud but not actually understand many of the words they are reading. Eventually reading becomes a bore.

They have difficulty taking meaning from what they read. As children progress through the school system, we expect them to read and research information themselves. Children with RLI find this very difficult. They may not be able to understand the text in terms of the vocabulary used and the grammatical structures within which it is presented. They require more time to work out the meaning of language and are less efficient at scanning for information.

Their written work will reflect their understanding of language. As with spoken language, written language relies on vocabulary and grammatical structures that the child understands. A child with RLI is unlikely to use vocabulary that they do not understand in their written work, nor will they use grammatical structures and markers that do not carry meaning for them.

They are less able to use linguistic clues to help with reading. When children read they are using a variety of clues to help fluency and predict the next word. Amongst these skills is the ability to make predictions about the likely next word, from knowledge of sentence structure and meaning within the sentence, and from the context of the story or text. Children with RLI do not have such well-developed knowledge of language and consequently will not be able to use prediction skills. They will rely more heavily on phonic clues to help predict the next word.

They have restricted language skills to help with planning of written text and stories. Again this reflects their own spoken language skills, which in turn reflect their knowledge and understanding of vocabulary and grammatical structures. More than this, children with RLI have restricted internal language, which is used to aid planning and problem solving. (Further discussion about this in relation to Vygotsky's theories of internal language is in Chapter 4.)

Chapter 3

Identification of children with understanding difficulties

What should you look for?

It is not always obvious when a child has difficulty in understanding spoken language. What follows is a collection of things to look out for. This set of descriptions is summarised as a photocopiable checklist at the end of this chapter (p. 23) for you to use with individual children.

Appearing not to listen

Children who have difficulty in understanding spoken language will eventually switch off from what is being said because they cannot interpret it. They may have good listening skills, but this ability on its own does not mean they are able to decode language. Often these children start off by listening and trying to make sense of what is being said, but eventually give up and become distracted. In certain circumstances the child may anticipate being unable to understand from previous experience, and not bother listening in the first place. For example:

> Ryan fails to look at the teacher as she introduces the lesson and gives out
> instructions for the task. He hangs back as the groups disperse, watches
> what his group start to do and then joins in.

Difficulties following instructions

The language of instruction is particularly problematic for some children, reflecting their difficulties with memory, sequencing and understanding concepts. Class instructions are often lengthy and as a consequence the children may be unable to remember all the elements of what is said. In particular they may retain just the first and last parts. Children may have additional difficulties with keeping the instructions in order, so the sequence becomes disrupted. Perhaps most crucial for children with language difficulties is that instructional language such as *before, after, when you have, only if* is particularly hard to understand. For example:

'You can put your books away after you go out for break', may be interpreted as 'Put your books away and then go out for break.'

Difficulties following discussion and story lines

Discussion and spoken stories may be hard for children to follow because a constant flow of language is being used. Children with understanding difficulties need a little additional time to interpret the words and ideas expressed. What tends to happen is that they have to dip out of the discussion while they interpret what has been said so far. When they turn back, they have missed some of it and will find it hard to catch up because of their linguistic limitations. Linguistically competent children and adults can plug the gap of information if a little bit is missed, but those with language difficulties – by their very nature – do not have the knowledge of sentence and word structures that enables them to make a good guess at what the missing information is.

> Zara tells the class about Viking boats when the discussion has moved from transport to what the Vikings did when they had invaded Britain.

Responses may be relevant but not accurate

Whilst young children will switch topics to suit them, as children reach school age they realise that it is usual to keep with the subject and issue being discussed. When a child's response to a question or contribution to a discussion is not accurate it is worth asking yourself why that might be. Sometimes the strangest of responses may relate to a misunderstood phrase or concept.

> Chelsea, when asked when she got her new shoes, replies, 'With my mum.'

> Sam tells the teacher about the little lambs in his book at home when the topic being discussed is signs of spring in the trees and flowers.

Difficulties understanding and using new vocabulary

As you introduce new vocabulary to the class, you may notice that some children do not ever seem to pick it up and use it in their own spoken or written work. For some children identifying unfamiliar vocabulary and acquiring the meanings of words is a huge difficulty.

> During the science lesson about evaporation, Harry is able to recall what happened to the water as it came out of the kettle and hit the cold glass, but his talking lacks the technical words you have introduced within the lesson and are expecting the children to have picked up. He says, 'The water got hot and came out like smoke and got all over the glass like rain.'

Use of simple, inaccurate or related vocabulary

Children acquire an extensive knowledge of words through exposure to the spoken word (see Chapter 1). This is further extended through the written word once they are literate.

Poverty of vocabulary results in the child being unable to express fully what they want to say.

Lara wants to tell you she saw a cement mixer, but uses the word 'lorry'.

Daniel wants to tell you about his garden shed, and calls it a 'hut thing'.

Difficulty understanding abstract vocabulary

Acquiring meanings for words which are not objects (nouns) or actions (verbs) is hard for some children. Abstract vocabulary requires a flexible interpretation of the meaning of the words and this causes them difficulty. This is revealed particularly when working on expressing emotions in indirect ways. For instance, in poetry a description of a 'sad house' brings together two words that do not normally relate to each other, and the meaning may be lost.

Problems understanding humour and jokes

Many jokes are based on words having more than one meaning or on fast interchange of vocabulary. These are linguistic skills that some children simply do not have. You may find that such children appear humourless, laugh late at jokes in response to the laughter of others rather than to the joke itself, or tell jokes that are not funny and have missed the point. (There is a developmental aspect to this skill, in that below the age of about 7 children are unlikely to be able to cope with word play, double meanings, and so on.) The following may be hard to appreciate:

'When is an English teacher like a judge? When she hands out long sentences!'

'When is a blue school book not a blue school book? When it is read!'

Why did the boy take a pencil to bed?
So he could draw the curtains!

Difficulties with sarcasm

Sarcasm, as already mentioned, requires a non-literal interpretation of what is being said. This is an advanced linguistic skill. As adults we often use sarcasm with older children. Those who do not understand it will pick up the literal meaning.

Teacher says with heavy sarcasm, 'This is a great piece of work, Darren', and Darren replies, 'Thanks, sir!'

Problems understanding text

We have seen that some children are able to read aloud, but when asked about it demonstrate that they have taken little meaning from it. This is particularly common for children with RLI.

> Ronan reads aloud the set of instructions on the worksheet and is asked to get on with the task. He says he does not know what to do, and is reminded that he has just read the instructions. He then turns the paper over to the blank side and asks where the instructions are.

Avoidance strategies

Children may develop avoidance strategies to ensure they are not challenged by the language in use around them. Some children volunteer for all the jobs – sharpening pencils, tidying books – and take a long time about it, in order to put off facing the language in the task ahead.

Some children will switch off from the talk and tasks, and become fidgety and distracted. This is not because they cannot sit still or attend to the task; rather it is a demonstration that they cannot interpret what is being said to or expected of them. Some children will develop this further into unacceptable behaviour as a way of avoiding the task in front of them. This strategy means they get themselves out of the setting and away from the demands of the language.

> Rory has sat quietly through the discussion, but once faced with the piece of work which he does not understand starts banging on the radiator next to his chair.

Withdrawal from interaction

When children cannot understand what is being asked of them, some will withdraw from interaction altogether. These children are particularly at risk of being overlooked as they are quiet and hoping not to be noticed – certainly not offering to join in with discussions – and frozen in fear if directly asked to contribute.

> Anya usually sits at the back, never puts her hand up, and when asked a question says she doesn't know. She shows signs of anxiety in group communication situations, but reveals some ability when the interaction is one to one.

Attitude of boredom

For children with significant difficulties understanding language, much of the school day may be confusing, frustrating and unintelligible. These children may present as being bored because little of what is around them is understandable, and they are unable to do much of what is asked of them. There is little motivation in listening to talk that you rarely understand, or in reading text that you can 'read' but take little meaning from. The intrinsic pleasure of reading for meaning and learning new things is rare for such children.

> Tia is always finding excuses for her written homework not being done. When it is art she completes it and hands it over eagerly.

Low self-esteem

Some children find themselves in a negative cycle of listening to what is being said to them, failing to understand it fully and then responding inaccurately. This may lead to low self-esteem, especially for those who have not developed strategies to help themselves when they do not understand (see Chapter 6). There is a higher than average incidence of mental health problems amongst children and adolescents with communication difficulties (see Chapter 4).

> Biancha, commenting on her school report, says, 'What is the point of having a go when all you get is A for effort and E for attainment. I'm useless!'

How to complete the checklist

In order to fill in the checklist you need a detailed knowledge of the child. It is often useful to ask the child's parents and key workers to help you complete the form. Consider each behaviour and decide whether the child exhibits it or not. It is useful to describe accurately the language demands that surround the behaviour. When thinking about the strategies used, try to be honest. It may be that none was used at the time. The very process of completing this form is likely to start a growing awareness of language demands on children.

Example

Behaviour	Describe the child's behaviour	What were the language demands at the time?	What strategies did you use? How successful were they?
Appearing not to listen	*Ruth was not looking at the speakers in group discussion and was distracting others.*	*Group discussion recapping story and what we thought about the characters.*	*Used Ruth's name to get her attention. Got the book out to give her visual support. Wrote characters' names on board.*

Using the form as part of formal assessment

This form does not take the place of formal language testing. You may choose to complete the form and then send it as part of a referral letter for further assessment. Those involved in formal language testing may use it as part of their information gathering about a child.

What to do with the information

Once the form is completed, take some time to look for themes and areas of difficulty which arise more than once. This will suggest where weaknesses are with regard to language.

If you have been able to collate some strategies that worked (and, just as usefully, that didn't work) this will give you some ideas about how to support this child with the demands of language in your setting. You can set targets using the areas identified and use the form to review the child's progress over time.

Receptive language checklist

Name: _____

Date: _____

Completed by: _____

Behaviour	Describe the child's behaviour	What were the language demands at the time?	What strategies did you use? How successful were they?
Appearing not to listen			
Difficulties following instructions			
Difficulties following discussion and story lines			
Responses may be relevant but not accurate			
Difficulties understanding and using new vocabulary			
Use of simple, inaccurate or related vocabulary			
Difficulty understanding abstract vocabulary			

Behaviour	Describe the child's behaviour	What were the language demands at the time?	What strategies did you use? How successful were they?
Problems understanding humour and jokes			
Difficulties with sarcasm			
Problems understanding text			
Avoidance strategies			
Withdrawal from interaction			
Attitude of boredom			
Low self-esteem			

Chapter 4

Links between receptive language impairment and behaviour

Receptive language impairment (RLI) may be very well hidden. The child presenting with behavioural problems may in fact have underlying language difficulties, which if resolved or supported will have a positive effect on behaviour. This chapter will set out the evidence for the links between these two difficulties and suggest some of the reasons for this. It will also examine some of the implications for children exhibiting behavioural problems whilst hiding a language difficulty. Strategies to support these children will be found in subsequent chapters.

Establishing the links

Perhaps one of the most misunderstood occurrences within the child population is the link between language and behavioural difficulties. It is estimated that 40 per cent of children with behavioural difficulties will have some aspect of language difficulty. The failure to appreciate the link between these two areas is reflected in the lack of co-ordination between the various services for these populations of children. There is gross under-resourcing of speech and language therapy services for children with emotional and behavioural difficulties (EBD).

Stevenson et al. (1985) found that children with speech and language impairment (SLI) at the age of 3 were at a higher risk of developing behavioural problems by 8. In children whose SLI had been resolved by the age of 8, the risk of developing behavioural problems was reduced by half.

Why do links exist?

Development of language and social skills

As a child's speech develops, their understanding of language and its uses develops concurrently. As discussed in Chapter 1, the ability to understand language normally comes before the ability to say things meaningfully. If a child has delayed understanding of language, it is probable that their ability to express themselves through talking will also be delayed. In the early years of life, learning the power of talking is very important. It gets you attention, you can ask for things, you can deny and refuse things, you can get more of something, and so on. Without language, children develop other means of making these things happen. This can be the start of using behaviour as a means to communicate. So whilst normally developing young children will assert themselves with behaviour – for instance take a toy from someone rather than asking for it – they gradually learn that there are other ways of dealing with this situation which involve language. Over time the behavioural communication will reduce and will be taken over by talking. Children who get off to a slow start in terms of understanding and talking, but whose language does eventually develop, may still have a pattern of using behaviour rather than talking. This is because they learned to interact through behaviour rather than through verbal communication.

He has discovered the power of talking.

Language and thinking

Young children talk out loud all the time. They are in fact doing their thinking out loud. This talk is a precursor to being able to think and solve problems in their head. It is also the beginning of the ability to modify their own behaviour by thinking through consequences. Thus a delay in language skills, both understanding and spoken, will result in delay in the development of thinking skills and problem-solving skills. Children affected are less able to think through how to solve a problem for which talking may be the solution. They also find it difficult to work out the consequences of their behaviour.

Language in a social context

Vygotsky's theories of language and learning emphasise the fact that for young children most effective learning takes place within a social context. Children for whom understanding, interacting and talking are difficult are at risk of failing to learn. From the age of 3 children are playing co-operatively together. As they do so, they are sharing, contributing ideas, instructing each other and modifying their play accordingly. Children who are unable to understand or contribute to the talking are at risk of being left behind by the group.

> Ethan is playing happily with two other boys with cars on the car mat. They start to talk about extending the play. One says,
>
> 'Let's take them off to the garage, because they're really dirty, aren't they, and they can go in the car wash.'
>
> As the boys move off to the garage, Ethan is left behind because he has not understood what they said, nor can he contribute ideas quickly enough to keep up with them.

Adult modification of behaviour

As children move out of infancy, adults tend to attempt to modify behaviour through talking.

> 'If you do that again there will be no sweets for a week.'

> 'Don't pull my hair because it really hurts.'

Children with understanding difficulties may fail to appreciate what is being said. They will probably understand that the person speaking had a cross face and raised their voice. For school-age children there will be an expectation that behavioural incidents will be talked through at length. For children with understanding difficulties this may simply add to the confusion.

Implications for children with RLI

Children with difficulties in understanding will learn to handle their problems in various ways. Sometimes the children will listen to the talking even though they are unable to understand. They will use socially acceptable ways of dealing with this:

- ☐ sitting quietly thinking about other things
- ☐ waiting for the talking to finish so they can ask their friend what is going on.

Sometimes the children will exhibit socially unacceptable ways of dealing with the situation:

- ☐ distracting other children
- ☐ calling out / playing the clown
- ☐ noise making, tapping, chairs rocking, and so on
- ☐ refusal to co-operate within the class.

Some will ask for help when they are stuck. These are often the ones with mild difficulties in understanding; they are able to tell you which part of what was said or read they did not understand. They can tell you that they did not understand the second instruction, or a particular part of a worksheet. Children with moderate and severe difficulties in understanding will find language so confusing that they cannot separate out the bits they do understand from the bits they don't understand. These children often do not, or cannot, ask for help. Instead they develop other strategies to cope with the language demands being made of them, and some use behaviour as an avoidance strategy. (See Chapter 3 for behaviours to be alert to.)

For some children the seemingly constant difficulties of coping with language at school may have an adverse effect on self-esteem. They feel foolish and self-conscious, particularly in front of their peers. These children may vote with their feet and become school refusers.

It is worth spending a few minutes empathising with these children. How often do adults choose to put themselves into situations in which they fully anticipate failure on a daily basis? On the whole adults make career and lifestyle choices in order to avoid such situations. Children have to come to school, an environment where the language demands will always be high.

Implications of poor spoken language for behaviour

As previously stated, understanding generally precedes talking. So it is with vocabulary items such as emotion words. Children with understanding difficulties often have a poor understanding of the vocabulary associated with emotions, such as *worried, excited, proud, scared, frustrated*. These children may find it very difficult to express themselves. This may lead to frustration which is expressed physically. It may also lead to reluctance to talk, sometimes interpreted as insolence.

The language difficulties commonly found in children with RLI (see Chapter 2) will affect the children's ability to recount events and incidents in which they have been involved. This may lead to misunderstandings both on the part of the staff and of the children. This needs to be taken into account when dealing with incidents in school and when disciplining.

Difficult, or experiencing difficulties?

There is a real danger of children with RLI being mislabelled. It is easy to categorise according to behaviour and to fail to look at the underlying situation. If the root of the behaviour lies within language processing, behavioural approaches to difficulties are not likely to be successful.

Consider the following descriptive labels and whether the behaviour is being caused by RLI.

Bad listener. Children who have difficulty in understanding language are at risk of switching off because, despite trying to listen, they cannot understand what is being said. This results in their eventually tuning out of the talking. Some children will sit quietly; others will exhibit unacceptable behaviours such as distracting others, messing around, chatting, interrupting, and so on.

Strange responses. When children have only partially understood what was said to them or asked of them, they may give some odd replies. They may have misunderstood a word or got the wrong end of the stick. It is normally possible to analyse an inappropriate response to a question and work out where the misunderstanding occurred. (This is examined in more detail in Chapter 3.) What needs to be borne in mind is that the children with RLI are not giving these inappropriate responses deliberately; instead they are operating on insufficient information and doing their best to engage in the interaction process.

Telling lies. Children with RLI will not always understand all that has been said to them. In some situations this may result in their apparently telling lies due to misunderstanding. It is also possible that when a child with RLI finds themselves backed into a corner – for example over an incident – they find it easiest simply to deny or agree with the person who is dealing with them.

Badly behaved. Children given instructions which they do not understand are unlikely to carry them out correctly. This does not mean that they are being wilfully naughty. The language in the task has proved a barrier to their being able to engage fully with the interaction or instruction.

Socially odd. A component of the full interaction process is not only understanding the words being used, but also understanding the non-verbal signs being given. Mature communication relies on our understanding the speaker's intentions as well as the words expressed. Some children have genuine difficulty in noticing and interpreting such information. These are known as pragmatic difficulties. These children appear gawky within the social context. It is very easy to mislabel their staring, interrupting, answering back, inappropriate humour, and so on as disobedience, cheekiness or just peculiar behaviour.

Lazy. This is perhaps the most commonly used description of children with unidentified RLI. The children appear lazy because they are unable to do what they have been asked to do and often will not speak up to say they have not understood. They appear unmotivated because they do not seek help. In fact they may eventually become highly unmotivated because they come across incomprehensible language in so many tasks. These children may rarely volunteer information or responses and may appear to be idle. They come across as uninterested in the lesson or discussion – often they will shrug their shoulders when asked for an opinion. (See Chapter 3 for the effect of RLI on self-esteem and school attendance.)

Violent behaviour. Some children will vent their frustration through physical aggression towards their environment, other children and adults. This aggression may stem from not being able to understand what is going on around them, not being able to understand what is being said to them, not being able to express themselves in the way that they would like, or from disillusionment on being told that they are stupid or lazy or being told to listen when they have listened but could not understand.

We have seen that 40 per cent of children with EBD have some form of language difficulty. Not all those children will have their language difficulties identified. When considering the nature of a child's difficulties, or talking to colleagues about a particularly challenging child, remember just how hard to detect RLI can be.

This is not to say that all children exhibiting the behaviours listed above have some form of RLI. Obviously some children do have behavioural problems that are not linked to language at all. It is also possible that a child with RLI may choose to exhibit behavioural problems alongside their language difficulties – unacceptable behaviour and RLI may co-exist, rather than one being a consequence of the other.

Chapter 5

Developing listening skills

Effective listening is the first essential skill in the interaction process. A failure at this level will result in misunderstandings and in inappropriate responses. Focusing attention on developing effective listening skills is the first stage in helping children with RLI. Addressing difficulties with listening may be sufficient to repair the communication breakdowns that otherwise occur.

This chapter takes a look at the development of listening and attention skills, and suggests a framework for assessing a child's level of listening. This leads to ideas for target setting. It also presents a practical framework for developing effective listening skills in the classroom.

Development stages of listening and attention

The ability to listen and give focused attention to talk is something that develops throughout the early years of a child's life. The following series of stages emphasises the subtle but significant changes that have to occur before a child can be considered an effective listener. Note that the age levels given here are approximate. (These stages are taken from Cooper, Moodley & Reynell, 1978.)

Stage 1 – during the first year of life

Extreme distractibility. The child's attention is held momentarily by whatever is the dominant stimulus. In effect young babies have no control over their attention. Whatever is the loudest or brightest stimulus will take their attention away from one thing and on to another.

Stage 2 – second year

Rigid attention. The child can concentrate for some time on a task of their own choice, but cannot tolerate any adult intervention. This is not an act of defiance. If the child is to gain from the task or object that has their attention, they need to shut out all other distractions.

Stage 3 – third year

Single-channelled attention. The child is becoming more flexible, and with an adult's help can transfer attention from their task to the adult's direction, and then back to the task. At this stage it may be necessary to get the child's attention by calling their name, tapping them on the shoulder, getting down to their eye level, and so on. With this help the child can move from attending to the task to attending to the speaker, and then go back to the task.

Stage 4 – fourth year

Single-channelled attention. The child still requires their full attention to be on a task, but they can now transfer attention spontaneously. So, for example, Sophie who is concentrating on drawing her picture will look up and listen when she hears you talking to her. She will gradually move to needing to look at the speaker only if the directions are difficult to understand.

Stage 5

Two-channelled attention. At this stage the child can listen to and act upon verbal directions related to what they are doing, without stopping to look at the speaker. They are ready to cope in class. For example, Kai who is trying to fix his car is able to listen to and carry out his mum's suggestion that he tries putting the wheel the other way round, without stopping to look at her.

Stage 6

Mature school-entry level. This is when integrated attention is well established and well sustained.

How to use the stages

Interpreting poor listening behaviour. These stages will help you to interpret children's behaviour when it comes to listening and attending. When a child does not appear to listen to what is being said, the following question needs to be asked:

Is the child **choosing** not to listen, or are they **unable** to listen?

A child at the early stages of attention control is not able to switch attention between tasks.

Effective control of attention develops over the first five or six years of life. Children in the Foundation Stage at school may still have a little way to go before they can be considered to have fully developed listening and attention control. Children with developmental difficulties, such as learning difficulties or language delay, are likely to have delayed attention and listening skills. It is unlikely that they will develop attention and listening skills that are ahead of their other levels of development. The age levels given in these stages are only an indication, and need to be viewed in the light of a child's overall developmental and learning profile. For instance, it would be unrealistic to expect a child who is still largely at stage 1 or 2 to be able to achieve in a setting where stage 5 skills are necessary in order to take part in the lesson.

The ability to attend to a task and cope with other stimuli is affected by a number of factors. Probably the most significant factor is the difficulty of the task. Here are some examples of how for adults levels of attention control may vary.

Single-channelled attention mode often comes in handy.

- You are on holiday, and find yourself in a foreign market place. You will be overwhelmed by the stimuli around you: the noises, the smells, the unusual things, the unfamiliar language. For a few minutes you are probably unable to hold a conversation. In effect you are like a child at stage 1 of the levels of attention: your attention is being held by the unfamiliar stimuli you are exposed to.
- You are at home and preparing a meal. You are cooking and supervising homework while listening to the radio. This is reflective of stage 6 of the attention levels.
- You are trying to read an article in a professional journal. You put yourself into single-channelled attention mode in order to concentrate, finding a time when there are not many distractions.

Reflecting on your own ability to listen and attend in differing situations helps you to understand a child's attention and listening skills. The other significant factor is emotional state. Ability to give focused attention, and subsequently listen, is affected by negative emotions.

The stages of attention are a great tool for assessment. It may be reported that 'Kira never listens to a word I say.' These stages help you to assess a child's ability to attend and listen. Through a period of observation and discussion with adults who are familiar with the child, it is possible to build up a picture of their skills. It is essential to gather information about the child's abilities in a variety of different learning situations.

- How difficult or absorbing was the task that the child was engaged in while you were trying to get their attention?
- How do you usually get their attention?
- Does it make a difference whether the child is in a group setting or in a one-to-one setting?
- Does the time of day make a difference?
- Consider the language demands within the situation (see also Chapter 3).

It is likely that through gathering this information, it will become apparent that the child is at varying levels of attention according to the factors listed above. This information will help you to set measurable and achievable targets for them.

Once the attention profile has been gathered, targets can be set. It is essential to have an accurate description of ability to listen and give focused attention before setting targets. For example:

> Josiah has rigid attention when focused on a task and shows no ability to 'listen and do'. An appropriate target for him would be to respond to the teacher using verbal and physical prompts to help him shift his attention from his task to the speaker.

Note that in normal development each stage can last for about a year. When setting targets it is essential that the child is not raced through what would normally take four or five years. When a child has moved from single-channelled attention at stage 3 to spontaneously transferring attention at stage 4, let them experience stage 4 for a while.

Other factors affecting listening skills

Our ability and desire to listen are affected by more than the developmental stage that we are at. Here are three other factors that need to be considered when describing a child's listening ability.

Hearing. If a child is suspected of having any difficulty in listening, it is very important that their hearing is checked. In some inner-city areas the incidence of conductive hearing loss (glue ear) in children is as high as 40 per cent. The critical factor for this group of children is that they do not learn to rely on auditory input because it is an inconsistent source of information: conductive hearing loss results in fluctuating hearing. These children may prefer to rely on the visual medium because it is consistent, and therefore they fail to learn to use auditory input – they do not learn to listen. If hearing loss is suspected, it is imperative that a referral is made for a full hearing test; medical intervention or hearing aids may resolve the child's difficulties.

Understanding spoken language. This area has been touched on in previous chapters. The link between understanding skills and listening behaviour is very strong. If a child cannot understand what is being said or asked of them, the possible consequence is that they will 'switch off' and stop listening. Some children will just daydream; others will exhibit less acceptable behaviour (see Chapter 4). These children will demonstrate behaviour that suggests they are not listening when in fact they have tried to listen, failed to understand and now have given up listening. As adults we can associate with this – consider your own behaviour when a TV documentary is too complicated, or a lecture is going over your head. You switch off the television, or let your mind wander. Your understanding has affected your ability to give focused attention to what is being said.

Motivation. Giving focused attention requires an act of will. If what the children are being asked to listen to does not interest them, or they fail to see the relevance to them, the likely consequence is that they will not bother to listen. Children for whom understanding is hard work need to be motivated to put the effort into listening and switched on to the subject being discussed – they need to see the relevance to them.

The child who does not listen is easy to spot in the classroom. But are we only seeing the tip of an iceberg in terms of their problems? If we focus on the poor listening behaviour only, we may miss the iceberg underneath that is the real problem.

A framework for developing listening skills

This framework provides a structure for developing effective listening skills for children in a school setting. It is possible to take parts of the framework in isolation, but to be most effective the stages should be followed through in order. This is imperative for children who have significant difficulty in listening to spoken language.

1. Identify the problem. It is important that the children know what they are working on. The problem needs to be named. The work may be called 'Being good listeners' or 'Good listening'. Always refer to elements of the work under the term you agreed on.

2. Discussion to develop strategies or rules. Children are used to having rules enforced upon them. The difference in this activity is that the children develop the rules themselves. They are more likely to use the rules if they are ones they have arrived at themselves and understand.

Your group listening rules will probably include:

- ☐ Do not fiddle or fidget
- ☐ Look at the person who is talking
- ☐ Think about the same thing as the person who is talking
- ☐ Listen with your ears
- ☐ Do not interrupt.

Here are some ideas for arriving at the rules you will probably require.

- ☐ *Group discussion.* You can simply introduce the subject of listening and ask the children to tell you what they think makes someone a good listener. Jot down their ideas and turn them into some rules or suggestions. This will be most effective with an older group.
- ☐ *Demonstrate poor listening.* To do this well you need two adults, A and B. This activity is introduced as one where the children have to watch A and let A know whether they have been a good listener or not. A asks B a question and then doesn't listen to the answer. The question needs to be open ended so that B can keep talking for a couple of minutes, for example:

  'What did you do at the weekend?'
  'What are your holiday plans this year?'

  For the purposes of this exercise B mustn't be put off by the fact that A is not listening. The children will need to see quite a lot of poor listening behaviour in order to be able to come up with the rules.

  Whilst B is talking, A shows some poor listening behaviour in an exaggerated way, so that the children notice. For example:

Look away from B	Interrupt B
Fiddle with things	Start talking about something else.
Start humming	

When the conversation has finished, turn to the children and ask them for their comments about A's listening. Ask them to be specific about how they know A was not listening. What was A doing wrong? What should A have been doing? Through this discussion you will end up with some rules for good listening that the children have discovered for themselves.

☐ *Use published resources*. Wendy Rinaldi's SULP (Social Use of Language Programme) contains some useful stories concerning social skills. She introduces characters such as Listening Lizzie and Betty Butting In. The stories help the children arrive at rules for developing good listening skills.

3. *Practise listening*. Use very simple activities. Listening activities include the following:

☐ Sound lotto on CD. The children listen to a sound on the CD and match it to a picture.

☐ Matching sounds together – shakers with different items in them, or musical instruments. One is played but not seen, and the children match it from a selection in front of them.

☐ Same and different games, in which the children decide whether two sounds (*p–p* vs *t–d*), noises (drum vs tambourine), words (*key* vs *tea*) or sentences (*The dog ran across the road* vs *The dog walked across the road*) sound the same or different.

☐ Giving simple instructions. With colouring sheets: 'Colour the car in yellow, colour the square red.' In PE: 'Run to the red mat, skip to the wall, hop to the window.' With building blocks: 'Put the red one on top of the blue one, next put the green one on top.'

☐ Finding games: 'Find me a red pencil, find me a blue book.'

Remember that for these children listening is hard, so the activity itself needs to be easy. The cognitive load is on the listening element of the activity. At the start of the activity draw the children's attention to the listening rules and which ones they will be using. During the activity use the rules to give positive feedback and to draw a child back to the task.

Example using sound lotto on CD

This would be a good introduction at the start of the activity:

'OK, children, we are going to practise our good listening today. We shall listen to the CD and find the picture that goes with the sound. Who can tell me whom or what we are listening to?

That's right, Josh, we are listening to the CD.

Where are we looking?

At me? No, we should look at the pictures.

What are we thinking about?

Yes, we need to think about the sounds.

Are we moving around or keeping very still?

That's right, we need to keep still to listen and then move to put the counter on the picture that we heard.'

During the activity specific feedback can be given:

'Remember to look at the pictures, Leo. That will help you listen to the sounds.'

'I can tell that you are thinking about the sounds you can hear. Great listening, everyone!'

---

4. *Monitoring of listening skills.* It is helpful for the children to receive feedback on the listening throughout an activity, as suggested above. At the end of an activity it is also useful to review how the listening went and to discuss the consequences of their listening:

> 'What happened when you didn't listen to the tape, Kyle? Yes, it meant you didn't know which picture to cover up, so you got that one wrong. That's why listening is so useful – isn't it?'

> 'What happened when you listened really carefully, Lisa? That's right, it meant you could think about the picture. Well done. Listening helps us get things right.'

5. *Evaluation.* As part of the monitoring process it may be useful to involve the children in evaluating their own skills. Using simple self-evaluation sheets will help the children reflect on their own ability and behaviour, and make clear what their next target will be. Some example sheets are provided at the end of the chapter for this (see p. 40). You may wish to devise your own in order to personalise them for the group you are working with.

Constructive evaluation needs to be honest. To encourage the children to say 'I wasn't sitting still and that meant I didn't listen very well', there needs to be an environment in which they will not be reprimanded for failure, but praised for honest reflection.

It will also be positive for the children to take part in evaluating each other. This can be done by asking one child to observe the group and to use a monitoring sheet to give specific feedback to their peers.

Talk about listening in groups

Throughout all these activities it is useful to talk about listening – why it is useful, when we use it, and so on – so that this skill is not seen as one that is only carried out when the teacher says 'We are working on good listening.' Here are some questions to form the basis of discussion:

- ☐ Why do we listen?
- ☐ What helps us to listen?
- ☐ What do we listen to?
- ☐ What happens if we don't listen?
- ☐ When do we need to listen?

Here is an example of a word storm on this subject with 7-year-olds:

Word storm with branches from a central box reading "What do we need to listen to?": jokes, computer, teachers, phone, my mum, police car, fire alarm, music, friends, TV

A good listening classroom

Teaching, particularly in large groups, relies on the pupils being able to give their attention to amounts of information that are often large. Chapter 6 considers the situation of children who cannot understand the language they have heard; our concern in this chapter has been to help children develop the skills to listen and gather in the information in the first place.

A good listening classroom will be one where the ability to listen is not assumed, but is recognised as a skill and is praised and rewarded as such. The classroom ethos will reflect the fact that many factors affect a child's ability to listen and give focused attention to what is being said. You as teacher will be able to alleviate some of these factors, or take account of them, within the classroom by such means as the following:

- ☐ Make efforts to reduce distracting or competing noises.
- ☐ Ensure the children can always see the face of the person who is talking.
   This will help them to concentrate, gain clues from the speaker (see Chapter 6) and give the speaker some feedback by showing that they are listening.
- ☐ Avoid activities involving lengthy periods of listening when the children are tired.
   A child's state of mind – especially extreme tiredness, excitement, fear or anxiety – will affect their ability to focus attention.
- ☐ Supplement what they listen to with visual props to help maintain their attention.
- ☐ Think carefully about the length of time during which children need to listen, particularly as work is introduced. Can this time be reduced, for example, by talking to different groups separately; or by talking one part through first, getting the children to do this, and calling them back to listen again later?

If good listening skills are to be put into everyday use, some children will need help transferring the skills and the knowledge of the rules into the classroom. Once the children have identified their rules and have started to practise their new-found listening skills in simple activities, it is crucial to help them make this transition. Children with language difficulties often have problems with the skill of generalisation (applying a skill or piece of knowledge learned in one area to another).

Within the classroom you can help in the following ways:

- ○ Display the listening rules on the walls.
- ○ Have listening prompts on the tables.
- ○ Use the same prompts to introduce a lesson – about what you are listening to, thinking about, and so on.
- ○ Ensure that all staff and volunteer helpers in the classroom are aware of the rules and the expectations of self-evaluation by the children.
- ○ Provide specific feedback during the lesson about the children's listening skills.
- ○ Have listening awards within particular lessons at the end of the day/week.
- ○ Involve the children in identifying the good listeners within their groups, and particularly those trying hard with the listening rules.
- ○ Present certificates of achievement for listening for those who find it particularly difficult, but are making progress.
- ○ Have a special corner where the emphasis is on listening. Activities here could include story CDs, sound CDs, musical instruments and the children's own recordings of voices for them to listen to and identify.
- ○ Use Circle Time to emphasise the listening rules.

Monitoring sheets for listening skills

As discussed earlier in the chapter, use of monitoring sheets is an essential part of developing effective listening skills. The sheets provide a visual prompt for the elements of good listening that are being practised. Before the activity or lesson commences, the sheet can be used as a brief reminder of the skills to be practised.

At the end the children are asked to evaluate their skills honestly using the sheets. The child who did not do well with the listening rules needs to know they will not be told off for this, otherwise they are unlikely to be honest in their self-evaluation. It may be necessary to praise the honesty of a child who knows they did not perform well. The child's evaluation provides you with valuable information about their own ability to reflect on their performance within a task. You can follow this up with discussion about the consequences of their success or otherwise.

Inviting the child to suggest an area to work on, or to give more focus to, will provide a useful start for subsequent activities.

Two different monitoring sheets are provided here (1 and 2). They are appropriate for different age and ability levels. Monitoring sheet 1 has space for evaluating four sessions.

The sheets may be completed using words to describe each listening rule, for example:

- ☐ All the time
- ☐ Most of the time
- ☐ A little bit
- ☐ Not at all

It may be more appropriate for the children to shade the box according to how well they thought they did. For example:

- ☐ Shade all of the box if they were sitting still all the time.
- ☐ Shade half the box if they looked at the speaker for some of the time.
- ☐ Leave the box blank if they were daydreaming throughout.

Some children can respond by giving themselves marks out of 10 for each rule. Others will simply need a tick or cross for each box (although this approach may be disheartening for a child who is struggling to carry out the rules).

Once the children have completed the sheets with you, you have a good opportunity to discuss what happened within the listening activity in terms of how well the child achieved. Point out, for example, that Marlon sat still and looked at the speaker, which helped him to think about his work and get it right. Sofia was fiddling with her pencil throughout and that may have been the reason why she couldn't answer some of the questions. Such discussions are important as they help the children to understand the significance of listening and why they should bother to do it.

Monitoring sheet 1

Sit				
Look				
Listen				
Think				

Next lesson, I need to think about _____

Date _____ Signed _____

Permission to Photocopy

- - - ✂ -

Monitoring sheet 2

Permission to Photocopy

Chapter 6

Developing strategies to help understanding

This chapter sets out suggestions for making the classroom a positive experience for those with RLI. It also details strategies for use in the classroom to teach and encourage children with RLI. There are responsibilities here for staff and children to apply, beginning with approaches for staff to develop.

A positive classroom ethos

We have learned that RLI may result in low self-esteem and a disengagement with learning and interaction at school. A positive classroom ethos with regard to RLI can change children's attitudes to school and learning, and indeed to themselves.

Children with RLI have only ever known a world that they partially understand. They do not know what it is like to understand spoken language most of the time; for them the world of language has always been a bit like being in fog. They may find it difficult to identify what it is they do not understand, and therefore find it difficult to seek clarification or ask for help. These children find themselves in the negative cycle of not understanding, guessing and failing shown in Cycle 1 on p. 42.

The positive classroom will engage with this difficulty and be based on clear roles and responsibilities such as these:

- ☐ As a teacher it is my job to help you understand.
- ☐ As a pupil it is your job to listen and tell me when you have not understood.
- ☐ In my classroom it is OK if you do not understand.

By developing this ethos and by giving children the skills and confidence to seek help, you can make the cycle more like Cycle 2 on p. 42.

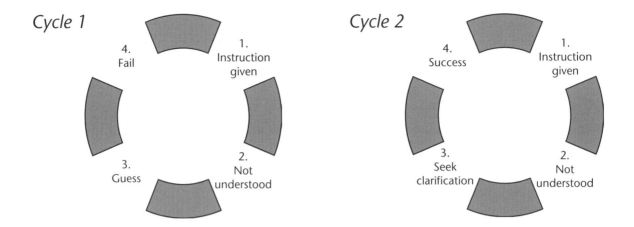

Maggie Johnson (2005) put forward ideas about **active listening**: children taking responsibility for their understanding difficulties and being given strategies to be able to help themselves.

We should aim for children to take responsibility for understanding a message, so that rather then guess or opt out, they acknowledge the difficulty and seek clarification.

Listening versus understanding

It is essential that the distinction between children not listening and children not understanding is fully understood and taken on board. Once it has been determined that a child can listen appropriately (stage 5 or 6 – see Chapter 5), there has to be an expectation that they are listening in class. However, no amount of 'good listening' will help a child whose understanding skills are very restricted. Similarly, once it has been established that a child has difficulties in understanding spoken language, there has to be an anticipation that they will not understand everything that is said and may need further support.

Children find it frustrating to be told they were not listening when in fact they had been listening but had not understood. This experience has serious effects on their willingness to ask for help in that classroom. Look at Carl's experience:

'I know I have to listen to give myself a chance of knowing what to do. I did listen, but I still didn't understand everything the teacher said. So I asked him and he told me that I should have been listening, then I would know what to do! It's so unfair. I was listening! I won't bother asking next time because I just get told off!'

A language-friendly classroom

The suggestions that follow are not rocket science! As adults we all know how to change our spoken language naturally. We do not speak to babies in the same way as we speak to our peers. Yet it can come as quite a shock to have to change the way we speak to children because their level of understanding is significantly below their chronological age. It is always worth keeping in mind what would help you to understand if you were in a country where you did not speak the language, or in a lecture on a subject you knew nothing about.

- ☐ Reinforce listening and giving focused attention. Remind the children of the need to listen (see Chapter 5).
- ☐ Modify your rate of speech. Children with RLI take longer than others to process the language they hear. Simply talking a little more slowly, pausing occasionally, makes a significant difference.
- ☐ Allow time after questions before expecting a response. Giving children a little extra time to think about the question and to formulate their response really helps. They will be more likely to give you a response than just shrugging and guessing. You may choose to be very directive about this; having posed the question to the group you may say:

'I am going to ask you, Harry, in a minute. Start thinking about your answer.'

You may ask the question, hold your hand out like a stop sign for a count of 5, then encourage the answer. This is a useful technique for children who dive in with an answer without having given it much thought.

- ☐ Be aware of the amount of talking. Can a 10-minute introduction be delivered in smaller chunks? Is it necessary for all the different groups in the classroom to sit and listen to all the instructions given to the groups before they set to work? Perhaps it is possible to give the instructions directly to the group concerned, reducing the chance of confusion and overload for the child with RLI.
- ☐ Establish the topic. Children with RLI often have difficulty with memory. Give them the category or topic into which they are to put the information being talked about. 'Filing' information in such a way helps to access what they already know about a topic, which aids retrieval of the information (see Chapter 7). It can be valuable to think about this in relation to your own needs in conversation or discussion. If the speaker launches into a topic without having established the subject, or if we come into a conversation halfway through, then as a listener we have to work quite hard to find out what is being talked about. For the child with RLI this is especially difficult.
- ☐ Consider the language you use. Children with RLI are unlikely to be able to understand complex sentence structures. Think about simplifying your language structures. It may help to think about the sort of sentences you would use with a younger child compared with those used with a teenager. Simply using shorter sentences may be valuable.
- ☐ Question words. Be aware that children find *why* and *how* question words hard to understand (and therefore to answer).
- ☐ Rephrase what you have said. Be prepared to give explanations in a few different and straightforward ways. But also be aware that too much language may flood a child with RLI with words and structures that they cannot decode.
- ☐ Consider the vocabulary you use. Introduce new words carefully. Refrain from using many new words or concepts during one lesson (see Chapter 7).

○ Avoid use of non-specific words such as *it*, *this*, *that*, and so on. For a child with RLI it helps to hear the specific noun again and again. This reinforces their learning of the word (if it is new to them). It is also an aid to their retaining and understanding the word.

○ Use non-verbal communication (see Chapter 1). When speaking to children with RLI it is enormously important to scaffold spoken language with non-verbal clues. The use of gesture, pointing, eye gaze (looking at what you are talking about) and facial expressions will all support the words and sentences being used.

○ Use visual information. Visual references help the child with RLI immensely. They aid the retention of information, and keep attention focused on the topic being discussed. Use of pictures, real objects, diagrams, moving images, and so on is a valuable support to the spoken word.

○ Ask 'Are there any problems?' This is part of the positive classroom ethos, accepting that some children may not have understood all that was said or has been asked of them. Permission is given to the children to say that they have not understood. This moves them from the negative cycle of understanding to the positive one.

The class can signal to you their understanding and readiness to tackle the task. You could try asking for thumbs up if they are ready to get going, thumbs down if they need some more help, and thumbs waving on the horizontal line for those with a problem. These signals are a great way for the teacher to ascertain quickly the group's understanding, and show the pupil with RLI that they are not the only one who may not understand.

'Are you ready to get going?'

There now follow strategies to teach and encourage the children themselves to use. The section is followed by some games and activities to elicit and practise the strategies.

Asking for help and seeking explanations

Children with RLI do not know what they do not understand. What they do know is that it doesn't make sense. Their experience up to the point of positive intervention may have been of confusion and failure. These children are aware that they are expected to respond to talking, and do so to the best of their ability – or opt out (see Chapter 4). The aim of this section is to break the negative cycle and give the children the skills they need to sort out their difficulties.

> **Scenario**
>
> You ask a group of children to colour a Christmas tree picture in green. You have forgotten to put out any green crayons on the table. What would the children do?
>
> It is quite possible that the child with RLI will be confused (that is normal for them) and either wait and follow the other children or pick up another colour, assuming that they had not understood properly. This is an example of the negative cycle at work. The child has guessed rather than taking control of the situation, as most able children would.

The principles underpinning the work towards a positive cycle of listening focus on problem solving:

☐ Accepting that there is a problem, identifying it, and doing something about it.

The communication problems that a child with RLI may come across are set out in the following chart. Next to each difficulty are some suggestions for asking for help.

Problems and strategies

Problem	Strategy
The speaker is too quiet.	'Please would you speak up?' 'I can't hear you.'
The talking is too fast.	'You are talking too fast for me to understand.' 'Please will you slow down?'
There is too much talking.	'You said too much.' 'I can't remember all that.' 'Will you say the last bit again? I can't remember what you said.' 'Please will you say it a bit at a time?' 'Can you write it down for me?'
Specific spoken words are not understood.	'I didn't understand this word …' 'What does … mean?' 'Can you use simpler words, please?'
The talking is complicated.	'May I have another minute to work it out, please?' 'Please will you give me a little more time?' 'Will you show me what you mean?' 'Can you put it a different way, please? I did not understand.'

These strategies may be discussed or read by the children and used as a guide or prompt. Encourage them to generate their own ways of asking for help using their own words. They are more likely to remember and develop confidence if the strategy feels natural to them.

How to work through the problem solving

Set up a scenario similar to the one above which you anticipate that the child with RLI will find easy to understand but impossible to comply with. When the children look confused, ask them if there is a problem. This gives them permission to say that there is.

Work together as a group to determine what the problem is. This may need a lot of prompting, but try to manoeuvre it so that the children eventually identify the difficulty themselves.

Ask the children what they could do about the problem. Again encourage them to use their own words to ask for help to solve the problem. These are the key questions for them to remember:

- ☐ Is there a problem?
- ☐ What is the problem?
- ☐ What can I do about it?

At first it is useful to practise this in activities which are very simple. This allows the focus of attention to be on developing the problem-solving skill and practising the clarification questions. Once the children are confident in the simple activities (which have been deliberately sabotaged for them to practise), there can be an expectation of starting to transfer the skills into the classroom.

Suggested activities

Worksheets. There are worksheets available (e.g. from Learning Materials Ltd) that provide an opportunity to give instructions that include a problem for the children to solve before they can respond correctly. The task might be to colour specific pictures, or add some features to a part of a picture. As you give the instruction, bring in a problem, for example:

- ☐ say it too quietly to hear, or too fast
- ☐ give too many instructions.

Screen games. Set up sets of familiar objects one on each side of a screen. Position yourself with the child/children on one side and you on the other. Give instructions, for example:

'Put the pencil under the red paper.'
'Draw a house on the white paper.'

As you give the instructions, bring in problems as suggested above. You can also sabotage this activity by not having the same items on each side of the screen and asking the children to do something that is not possible, for example:

'Put the ball under the red box' – when in fact the children
only have a blue box, or no ball.

Deliberate mistakes. Puppets are really helpful for introducing the ideas of mistakes and humour. Your puppet can be used in at least two different ways. The puppet may have difficulty saying the right things. Can the children tell him when he gets it wrong and help him? For example:

The puppet says, 'Look at the boy with the book', pointing to a girl with a book.

Alternatively you can give the puppet instructions which he cannot do – what you said was too fast, you gave too much information, you used the wrong words, the instructions were too complicated, and so on. The puppet just looks confused or gets it wrong. Can the children help?

Game to encourage discussion about asking for help. Use the prompt cards provided (p. 48). Place the cards face down on the table in front of the group. Ask a child to take a card and read out what it says. The child then has to decide what they would say or do if they were confronted with that problem. You may need to give them a real example of the difficulty if they can't think what is meant. The other members of the group listen and give some different responses to the problem. You may decide that the group has to come up with three different things to say to deal with the problem. Or, to make it into more of a game, you could ask another child to roll a dice. The number rolled determines how many solutions the group must generate for that problem. Once the discussion about one card has finished, another child selects a new card from those on the table, the dice is rolled and the problem solving begins again.

It is very valuable for children to hear that other people face problems with understanding, and for them to listen to each others' ideas for solving a difficulty.

The aim of all the activities is to provide opportunities for the children to practise identifying problems with what they hear and asking for help with this. At first they may only be able to say 'I don't get it', 'I don't understand' or 'What do you mean?' For children with severe RLI this is a huge step forward. Through coaching and questioning you will be able to refine the question or the request for help to those suggested in the Problems and strategies table on p. 45.

Getting the strategies into everyday use

Once you are confident that the children have some phrases to use when they are stuck, it is appropriate to expect them to start using those strategies in class. Preface lessons with reminders of what the children should do if they do not understand. Make a point of praising children when they ask for clarification of something you have said. This will build assurance in the children that it really is acceptable to ask for help.

On occasion, have a discussion point around subjects such as these:

- ☐ the use of clarification strategies
- ☐ what happens if the children don't ask for help
- ☐ what happens when they do ask for help
- ☐ what holds them back from asking
- ☐ how they feel when they understand and get the work right.

Visual prompts and reminders on the walls and on a child's desk will all help to reinforce the message that as a teacher you expect the children to tell you when they do not understand.

Strategies for tackling written work

So far the emphasis has been on seeking clarification of spoken language. What does the child do when faced with written work they do not understand? The child with RLI is likely to guess or give up. Through learning some strategies they can achieve some independence in their work, developing less reliance on adult assistance to complete the task.

Discussion prompt cards

There has been too much talking	Speaker says words you don't understand
You can't remember all that has been said	The teacher is talking too fast
You can't hear what is being said	The words are too complicated
You don't know what to do next	You feel rushed and panicky

DIY (*Do It Yourself*). It is valuable to have discussions with the group about what they do when they are stuck with written work. After being given some support, children should gain a range of strategies.

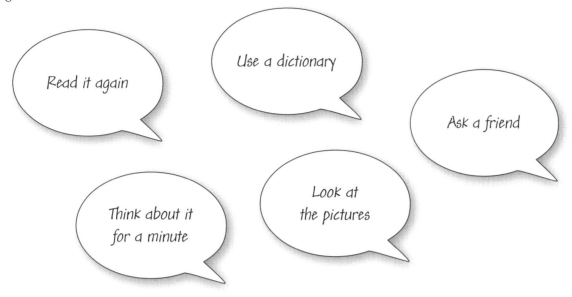

DIY is a great way to help the children feel they are taking control, and no longer passively stuck with no way of helping themselves. You will probably need to practise each of the strategies suggested in turn, in simple activities at first.

Key questions to be asked during the activity:

- ☐ Are you stuck?
- ☐ What can you do to help yourself?
- ☐ How did you work that out?

You need to praise the use of strategies suggested:

'That was great! You worked that out because you looked it up in the dictionary.'

'I saw you talking to Matt about that. Did it help to ask him? Well done for doing some DIY.'

A worksheet is provided for children to use (see p. 50). Invite them to write down what they will do to help themselves if they are stuck with written work.

Visual prompts around the classroom and work areas are very useful for the children. They emphasise the message that it is OK if you don't understand and that there are things that you can try in order to help yourself.

Detective work. The emphasis in detective work is on looking for evidence. You may find it useful to discuss with the children what detectives do, and how they solve problems.

This activity is particularly helpful for reading comprehension and for inferential understanding of text.

DIY

What can you do if you are stuck on written work?

Start with simple comprehension pieces, just two or three lines of text long. Ask one or two questions on each. Your key prompts through the activity will be:

- think
- look
- look for clues
- look for evidence
- use what you already know about a situation.

The children should read the text and the questions. They try to answer the questions by being good detectives and looking for the evidence. It is a good idea for the children to underline or highlight the evidence that supports an answer.

The questions for you to use could include:

- How do you know that?
- How did you work that out?
- What would you do?
- What do you already know about that topic?
- Show me the evidence.

This work can be done as a large group, using big books or enlarged texts which the children can mark with their evidence. If done individually, use sheets that they can highlight.

Once the work has been practised in simple activities, expect the principles to be applied in all classwork when appropriate. Preface tasks with a brief reminder of the principles of looking for clues and the need for the children to show how they arrived at their answer. Praise the children when they provide you with proof or evidence for their answers and let them know that this is what you expect of them.

Use of visual prompts in the classroom is a valuable reminder. It is worth thinking of a pictorial symbol that may be used to symbolise 'Detective work' – perhaps a magnifying glass, or a police officer looking for evidence.

Summary

This chapter has presented techniques for use by the teacher and other adults to help children in the classroom. It has also put forward strategies to be taught to the children. These strategies will become part of the child's own toolbox for coping at times when they do not understand. Through encouragement and praise of such strategies, the children will gain independence in their learning, and gain in self-esteem and life skills.

Chapter 7

Working on vocabulary

During their first six years of life children will learn the meaning of over 14,000 words. Once understood, these words find their way into the child's speech. Many children have a poor vocabulary. Children with RLI frequently have significant problems with vocabulary. Here are some common types of vocabulary error:

- ☐ Child uses the wrong word, but it is close in meaning:
  Peg for coat hanger, *nail* for screw.

- ☐ Child describes the word:
  'You know when you go in the water' for *diving*.

- ☐ Child makes up a word:
  Wrist collar for cuff on a shirt.

- ☐ Child uses non-specific words:
  It, this, that, her, him, them, over there, thingy, whatsit.

- ☐ Child uses a gesture to support or replace the spoken word:
  Mimes using a screwdriver whilst trying to think of the word.

This chapter will consider how children acquire new vocabulary, and then suggest activities to improve their skills. Finally, some thoughts are presented on how to select the vocabulary to teach children with significant vocabulary deficit.

The chapter ends with a checklist to assess your strategies for helping children with RLI (see p.63).

How we learn new words

The learning of new words involves gathering phonic information and semantic information about a word. In other words, there is a need to know what the word sounds like (**phonics**) and what it means (**semantics**). When a new word is heard, we are able to break it into its constituent parts and store that code of sounds or **phonic representation**. This is essential for the recognition of familiar words and for the retrieval of the sounds needed to say the word.

When we hear a word, a judgement has to be made about whether we recognise it or not.

The recognition of the word is dependent on the listener having correctly stored the sounds that make up the word. If the word is familiar, the listener accesses the semantic information stored and understands the word. If the word is not familiar, the listener must store the phonic representation or sound properties of the word accurately, and then start gathering some meaning about the word.

It is easy to see that if the listener has not stored the sound properties of the word accurately, there may be some inappropriate consequences:

- ☐ Confusion may arise when trying to make a judgement about whether the word is familiar or not.
- ☐ Similar sounding words may become confused.
- ☐ The meanings of words do not get stored with the correct phonic representation.

Having stored the phonic properties of a word, the child needs to gather some meaning for the word. It is rare for children to be given definitions of words to learn and remember (except in technical and educational settings). Where does the developing child get the information?

Children will acquire meaning through frequent exposure to the word within linguistic and physical contexts. From infancy children are able to gain information from linguistic placement of a word (see Chapter 1). They will recognise the place of a verb from a noun, for instance, and will gradually detect adjectives as describing nouns, and so on. Probably more important, however, is the need to hear the word in a physical and meaningful context. As the child hears the word – in association with certain objects, events, emotions, and so on – they gather the meaning of the word around the phonic representation of it. In young children the information they gather will at first be patchy and incomplete. They are likely to overgeneralise a meaning. For example, a young child will think that all vehicles are known as cars. They may restrict the meaning of a word – for example think that only their car is known as a car. Over time and repeated hearing of the words in different contexts, the child will add to and amend their understanding of a word.

It is worth recalling how as an adult you were able to learn some new words as they came into use. Take for instance the term *global warming* and the political word *spin*. Did you get a dictionary definition of these, or did you gather information as you heard them used within a meaningful context?

The theory behind the acquisition of vocabulary leads to a focus on two main elements of vocabulary storage: developing accurate phonic representations and semantic storage.

Activities for phonic storage

These activities centre around ensuring that the child has stored the right sounds that make up the word (the phonic representation). The ability to segment and store words in this way is called **phonological analysis**. Difficulties with phonological analysis have detrimental effects on speech sound development and literacy skills, as well as on vocabulary learning. The key questions that will support phonological analysis and storage of new vocabulary are these:

- How many syllables are there in the word?
- What sounds can you hear in the word?
- What does it start with?
- What does it rhyme with?

For some children it may be necessary to practise these skills in isolation. The following are a few ideas for this. (See also Liz Baldwin, *I Hear with My Little Ear*.)

Syllable work

- Clap the syllables for their name.
- Jump through hoops for the number of syllables in a picture you show them: for example elephant, crocodile, monkey, and so on.

Initial sound

- Help the child hear the similarities in the word by having a bag full of things starting with the same sound. Get them out one by one, for instance: pig, pencil, paint, pizza, paper. Ask the child to tell you what sound they start with. Encourage them to say the words and listen and feel the first sound they can hear. Can they think of any other words that start with the same sound?
- Play Odd One Out with initial sounds. Have two items beginning with the same sound and one starting with a different sound. Name them all together and then see if the child can identify which two go together. Be careful to emphasise that you are putting them together on the basis of what they sound like and not what they mean. Throughout the activity encourage the child to say the words out loud.

Sounds they can hear

- Say the word with the child, and encourage them to tell you what sounds they can hear, for example: *garden*. They will probably identify *g*, *d* and possibly *n*. Can they tell you whereabouts in the word the sound comes (beginning, middle or end)? Help the child who struggles with this to break the word into syllables and tackle each one separately; for example: *croc-o-dile*.

○ Using the same principles, you can encourage the child to link this to letters as an introduction to being able to spell the word. As the child tells you what sound they can hear, you write it down, or encourage them to find the correct letter from a selection of wooden, foam or magnetic letters in front of them. Obviously working in English there will be lots of anomalies with regard to the spelling, but these can be briefly explained. Remember that the focus of the activity is to build up the skills of phonic analysis for spoken words. Once the child has identified the consonants, you can fill in the remaining sounds. The child will find great satisfaction in moving towards spelling an unfamiliar word.

Activities for semantic storage

The work on semantic storage centres on gathering appropriate and salient information regarding the phonic representation of a word. The four key elements have some related questions that can be posed to help the children gather the correct information.

Category   What group is it in?
    What word family does it belong to?

Function   What does it do?
    What is it for?

Attribute   What is it like?
    What does it look like?

Location   Where would you find it?
    Where is it?

A visual aid for a word is particularly useful. The Word web diagram (p. 56) enables them to place the word in the centre and gather information around it to support their visual memory. Each question can be addressed and information can be recorded.

Completed Word web for 'warrior'

Some children will not be able to answer the questions suggested adequately, and will need to take a step back initially. You should get them to practise the questions in isolation from each other so that they become familiar with the type of information each question requires.

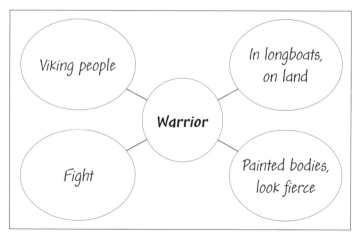

Word web

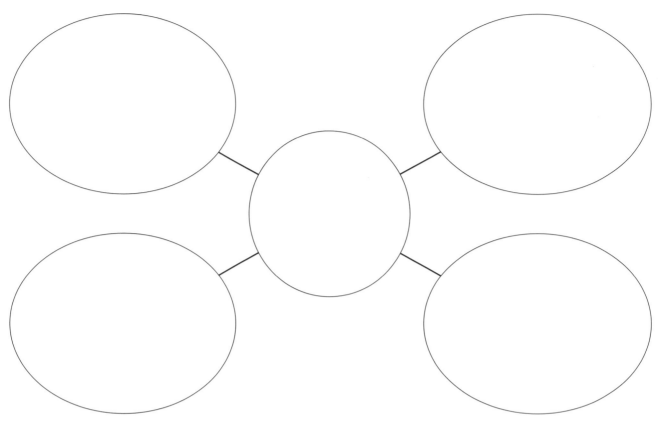

Permission to Photocopy

Word web

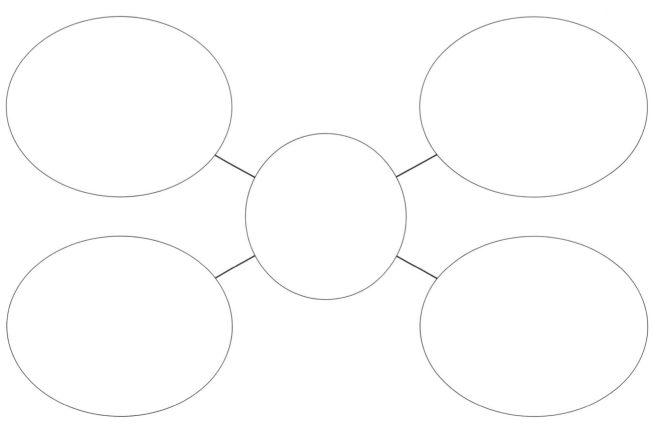

Permission to Photocopy

Breaking down the questions

Category questions

1. Find pictures or objects and toys in early, well-known categories, such as furniture, animals, transport, toys, food, clothes. Name the items and talk about why you have put them together. Give the category name and encourage the child to understand it. Can they think of other things that would fit? Give clues if the child is unsure.

2. Using sets of similar objects or pictures, introduce some rogue items that do not fit into the category. Play Odd One Out. Encourage the child to talk about the similarities and differences between the items and to use the category names if they know them. If they are unsure, give them the category name and support them in saying it with you.

3. Scatter cards from several different categories in front of the child. Play a pairing-up game in which they put two pictures together and say the category name; for example, *sock* and *glove* are clothes; *grass* and *flower* are plants. The child may not know the official category name and will describe it instead. The important thing is that they can do the categorising and explain the links between the items.

Function questions

1. Place some items in a drawstring bag. Invite the child to take one out and say what they do with it, or what it is for. If the vocabulary for the action is hard, ask them to mime it for you while you give the language.

2. Put out a selection of pictures or items in front of the child. Play a describing game, but give them only function information – for example, 'They are for cutting' (scissors). After the type of information to be given has been demonstrated, the child can try to give you the function of an item while you guess what the word is. Make this harder by giving the function of something that you are thinking about.

3. Brainstorm items that all have a similar function: 'Let's think of some different things we can cut with'– for example scissors, knife, lawnmower, clippers, razor. You can give points for the number of words the children can think of, or for thinking of words that no one else has thought of.

Attribute questions

1. This is best started with real objects so that children experience tactile information. You will need to prompt with questions such as these:

   For a teddy
   ☐ 'What does it feel like?' ☐ 'What is on its face?'
   ☐ 'How big is it?' ☐ 'What colour is it?'

2. Put out a selection of pictures. Describe the attributes of the picture. The children guess what it is. Once they are familiar with the sort of information being shared, they can try describing a picture to their friends for them to guess.

3. Play the pairing game: children pair up two pictures because of visual similarities – for example colour (banana and sun), number of legs (table and horse).

4. Play the Odd One Out game, with two items that clearly belong together and a rogue item. Can the child select the odd one and tell you why the other two go together?

Location questions

1. Consider common locations, such as school, home, the park, on holiday. Look at pictures of such scenes, or go to the real place or imagine it. Start naming items you can see that are commonly associated with the location. Make sure the child can name the location. Alternatively the child could draw a picture of the place and put into it ten things they usually see there.

2. Introduce the idea of rogue items, perhaps into the pictures that you are drawing – for example, draw a scene of a beach and include a computer. Can the child detect the item, tell you that it is in the wrong place and say where it is normally found?

3. Play a quick-fire question game. You say a location and the child has to tell you one thing commonly found there – for example farm, kitchen, swimming pool, moon.

Bringing it all together

Once a child is familiar with the questions and the type of information needed to answer them, they will be able to think about categorisation across the question types. The pairing-up and odd-one-out games can focus on any of the questions. The child should be encouraged to think about which question is being considered when looking at the similarities and differences of the meanings in the words.

Example

You pair up toothbrush and towel because they are in the bathroom (location).

You then pair up socks and pencil because they are both blue (attribute).

Next you pair train and plane because they are forms of transport (category).

Finally you pair phone and CD because you listen to them (function).

Resources for this work are in *Semantic Connections* and *Semantic Links* (Stass Publications).

Making it real

The children will find it helpful to have the questions they need in order to gather meaning in front of them. The Word web (p. 56) can be used by the children to research the meanings of words independently, or to reflect on what they know about a word. Patchy understanding will surface and enable the teacher or the children to fill in the gaps.

The spinner (p. 59) may be used to revise semantic knowledge of a word with a group. Set the word on the table in front of the group. They take turns to spin the spinner and answer the question it points to. This activity will help the teacher identify any areas of understanding that the children have not fully grasped, or are confused about. Photocopiable cue cards are also provided for use with the children (p. 60).

Word spinner

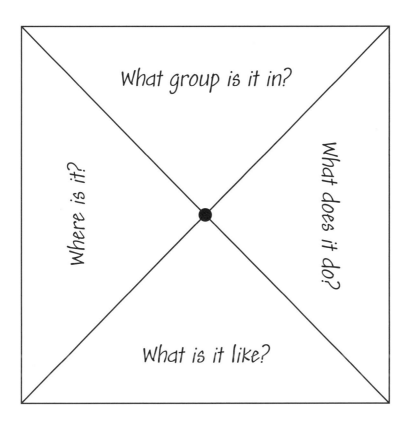

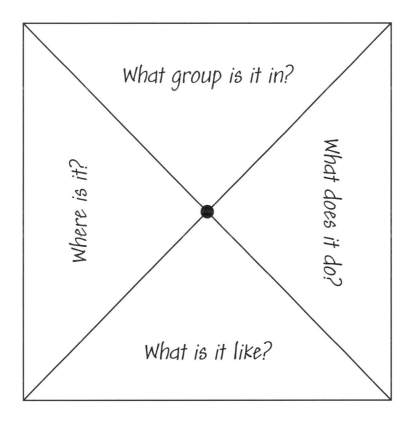

Cue cards: semantic and phonic storage

What group is it in?	What does it do?
What is it like?	Where is it?
How many syllables are there?	What sound does it start with?
What other sounds can you hear?	What does it rhyme with?

Visualisation

Children with RLI often have stronger visual skills than auditory skills for storage and recall. Visualisation provides a method of recording meaning. It involves providing the child with a large version of the word being discussed. After talking together about the meaning of the word, this activity gives the child the opportunity to represent its meaning within and around it. Provide the child with a worksheet showing a chosen word in large type. It is useful to make the lettering hollow as it allows the child to draw within the letters if they want to. Allow the child to make representations of the word in and around the letters. For example, the word *absorption* could be represented by the word standing in a puddle with some of the water being absorbed by the letters. The word *Viking* could be represented by the word inside a Viking longboat.

This type of activity may be used by all children to show what they know about a word, concept or emotion. It is an excellent way to revise the meaning of words. Because the work involves drawing, many RLI children will not see this as difficult – although giving the right meaning for a picture might be challenging for them. The completed sheets make good visual displays and are a way of getting parents involved with the vocabulary being used in class.

You could use large versions of words for children to copy and create word pictures during wet play or sand play.

How to select vocabulary

When faced with a child with poverty of vocabulary, it can be a daunting prospect to decide which words to teach the child first. There may be thousands of words missing from their lexicon, in comparison to that of most children of similar age. Where do you start?

Pre-teach subject-specific vocabulary

When lesson planning, and in particular when approaching new topics or areas of the curriculum, you will have identified some of the new vocabulary to be introduced. It will greatly help the child with RLI to have some exposure to those words before they come up within the lesson. The experience of having heard something before, even if it is not fully understood, is beneficial. Consider playing some phonic games with the new vocabulary to help lay down some good phonic representations. If the child is able, or has support at home or in school, you could give some of the new words to them to research so that they can complete a word web for them (see p.56). We all learn words through using them. If we teach words to a child who is unlikely to use them regularly or soon, those words are likely to be lost. By teaching words that are about to be used in class we are giving the child relevant vocabulary. This in itself will aid storage and recall.

Vocabulary the child does not understand

A knowledge of the child, and analysis of the words they do not understand, will give you a list of words that it would be useful to teach them. For example, in their reading book you may come across words that a child can read but does not know the meaning of. Keep a list as your basis for words to use with the child. You may find instruction words in, for example, PE that the child cannot follow, or technical words in science. Do not forget to emphasise the phonic properties first and then build up semantic knowledge.

Vocabulary the child does not use

When you are talking to children with RLI and other language difficulties, it is always useful to have a pen and paper ready to jot down any comprehension problems or to note any difficulty they have in using the right words when talking. These notes can form the basis of another list of words to work on with the child. For example, the child says *moon* for star. It is helpful to consider the phonemic properties of both words and then to do two word webs, one for each word. You can discuss with the child how similar the word webs are, and then consider the important differences.

Vocabulary the child identifies

Some children are able to identify some specific words they do not understand. (This may have been one of the targets you addressed in Chapter 6.) These children find it useful to have a notebook in which they can write down the word they do not understand. They can be encouraged to ask adults to explain the word, or to research the word themselves, using questions from the four key semantic elements (see p. 55) as a prompt. Again, do not forget the importance of the phonic properties of the word. As children become more able with print, they may be able to read and spell a word using visual memory but still be unable to recall it for talking, because the phonic representation is not accurate. Simply encouraging the child to say the word several times over is helping them to store it ready for recall.

Conclusion

This book concludes with a self-evaluation checklist. In many ways this serves as a summary of the content of the book, encouraging you to reflect on listening skills, messages conveyed by behavioural difficulties and the understanding of spoken language in your classroom. The checklist provides you with an opportunity to think about the strategies you use and those you encourage in your own work with learners. It is intended for personal use, but may also be helpful to use with a mentor, team leader or as part of a whole-school consideration of language in the classroom.

The aim of this book has been to provide information about the nature of receptive language difficulties and to suggest some strategies for use by both learners and their teachers. Honest self-evaluation and reflection, and incorporation of some of the strategies suggested will be of great help to a group of children whose needs may so easily go unnoticed.

Classroom practice checklist

Language strategy	Do I use the strategy? If yes, how?	Effect on children's performance
Do the children know about good listening rules?		
Is there opportunity to practise listening as a separate skill in my classroom?		
Are the listening rules reinforced through praise?		
Do I have listening awards?		
Are all staff aware of the rules for listening?		
Do I involve children in the evaluation of their own listening performance?		
Do the children feel confident in asking for help when they need it?		
How do I gauge a group's readiness to work independently on a task?		
Do I have visual prompts around the classroom for comprehension strategies?		
Do I reinforce and praise evidence-based answers?		
Do I praise children when they seek clarification?		
Do I introduce new vocabulary with attention to the phonic properties of the words?		
What strategies for semantic storage do I encourage?		
Do I make a note of children's comprehension and spoken errors?		
When faced with behaviour problems, do I consider the possibility of an underlying language deficit?		

Further sources of information

References

Baldwin, Liz (2007) *I Hear with My Little Ear*, Cambridge: LDA

Cooper, J., M. Moodley & J. Reynell (1978) *Helping Language Development*, London: Edward Arnold

Johnson, Maggie: *Functional Language in the Classroom – and at Home!* (2005) Manchester Metropolitan University Commercial Office
Tel: 0161 247 2535

Rinaldi, Wendy Social Use of Language Programme, Books for Professionals in Special Education, PO Box 176, Cranleigh, GU6 8WS
Tel: 01483 268825

Stevenson, J. *et al.* (1985) 'Links between Behavior and Language', *Journal of Child Psychology and Psychiatry and Allied Disciplines*, vol. 26, 215–230

Vygotsky, L www.english.sk.com.br/sk-vygot.html

Useful contacts

Afasic

Charity for people with communication difficulties.
1st floor, 20 Bowling Green Lane, London, EC1R 0BD
Tel: 020 7490 9410; Helpline: 0845 355 5577;
email: info@afasic.org.uk; website: www.afasic.org.uk

ICAN

Educational charity for children with speech and language difficulties; training for parents and professionals; numerous factsheets.
Central Office, 8 Wakley Street, London,
EC1V 7QE
Tel: 0845 225 4071; email: info@ican.org.uk;
website: www.ican.org.uk

Learning Materials Ltd

Learning Materials Ltd, Dixon Street, Wolverhampton, WV2 2BX
Tel: 01902 454026; fax: 01902 457596;
e-mail: learning.materials@btinternet.com
website: www.learning.materials.btinternet.co.uk

Royal College of Speech and Language Therapists

Professional body promoting excellence in practice; influences health, education and social care policies.
2 White Hart Yard, London, SE1 1NX
Tel: 020 7378 1200
email: info@rcslt.org
website: www.rcslt.org

Stass Publications

Semantic Links and *Semantic Connections*
These and other publications are available from Stass Publications, 44 North Road, Ponteland, Northumberland, NE20 9UR
Tel: 01661 822316; fax: 01661 860440
email: stass@stass.co.uk
website: www.stasspublications.co.uk

Talking Point

Aims to provide a one-stop shop for professionals and parents.
www.talkingpoint.org.uk